Peering Into Technology Coaching: Meeting 21st Century Teacher Needs

Virginia Richard
Kay Teehan

Graphic Arts Designer: Alex Harris
Layout Editor: Alex Harris

ISBN: 978-0-6151-7742-7

© by Virginia Richard & Kay Teehan

Acknowledgements

For our parents who were the best coaches we have ever had.

To all the little angels who read this book over and over again (you know who you are)!

Table of Contents

Forward by Karen Seddon
Page 7

Prologue: A Glimpse of the Past
Page 9

Chapter 1
    What is Technology Peer Coaching?
Page 17

Chapter 2
    Benefits of Technology Peer Coaching
Page 27

Chapter 3
    Implementing Technology Peer Coaching
Page 39

Chapter 4

    Why does Technology Peer Coaching Work?

Page 53

Chapter 5

    What Characteristics are needed to
    be a Technology Peer Coach?
                                Page 65

Chapter 6
    Peer Coaching Models
                                Page 77

Chapter 7
    Administrator Support
                                Page 89

Epilogue: Supporting 21st Century Teaching and Learning
                                Page 99

Bibliography
                                Page 101

Appendix A

NSDC's Standards for Staff Development

                                Page 105

Appendix B

21st Century Standards and Skills
                                Page 109

Appendix C

21st Century Professional Development
Page 111

Appendix D

The Coaching Cycle
Page 113

Peer Coaching Resources
Page 115

About the Authors
Page 117

-Forward-

As a veteran educator who has seen the difference between the "egg carton" syndrome of the past and our present collaboration opportunities, I am very excited to see a comprehensive, yet fluid account of creating a school environment that works. At the heart of everything we do as educators, is our desire to do what is best for our students. Virginia Richard and Kay Teehan have written with passion and that special personal touch that will encourage, equip and empower teachers to implement the Technology Peer Coaching model in their classrooms. As Technology Peer Coaches begin to make an impact at their schools, student achievement will increase.

Teachers who are excited are contagious in the classroom and students are naturally encouraged to flourish in a positive environment. Understanding the secret of peer-to-peer coaching enables our teachers to make a true impact on their campuses and beyond. As more and more teachers understand the gift of sharing, students always benefit.

One of the areas that excite me the most is that teachers reading this book will be able to have a tangible way to "pay it forward." When one teacher touches another and another "pays it forward," the impact is exponential over time. Impact is not limited to our own campuses.

Teachers are becoming members of online learning communities and collaborative projects that touch the lives of students across the nation and even the world. The nuggets shared in this book will enable them to empower other teachers to reach their potential with protocols and tips in a professional development model that really works.

Playing the TIG© makes the journey into Technology Peer Coaching fun. The Technology Integration Game gives all participants an opportunity to win and affords us the opportunity to understand our roles in a uniquely American way. Take a swing and be sure to "pay it forward" to all teachers you know!

By Karen Seddon
Educator and Consultant

-Prologue-
A glimpse of the past…

Education has faced dramatic changes in the past 20 years. Educational professionals who have been teaching for over 20 years have eye witnessed the unfolding events that began in the 1980's with the *A Nation at Risk* report to the president on the state of American education. The report took a long hard look at how American education stacked up against other countries in terms of student scores on testing, number of college graduates in essential fields of study such as engineering, science, and technology. The account went on to give grave predictions of future decline if steps were not immediately taken to change the way we educate our children. While the report was a sobering look at a system in failure, it was not that much of a surprise to those of us who were in the classroom at the time.

Teachers knew instinctively that education lacked standards and goals and was largely being driven by textbook companies and the newest fads such as "open concept" or "new math". It became inevitable that politicians would step in to remedy the problem with the establishment of state standards, goals, and benchmarks and the obligatory testing to make sure the standards were being met. National legislation in the form of No Child Left

Behind promised that all schools would make adequate yearly progress towards success. Teachers throughout America applauded that education was finally becoming a front row topic in importance but also shuddered at the thought of politicians dictating what, when, and how students should be taught.

If the truth were known, education was broken and in need of repair and teachers did not have the means to fix the problem themselves. Part of it was because educators as a whole lacked a shared vision of what the American education should look like.

Professional development was ineffective and even absent in many school districts across the country. Leadership in the schools was mostly appointed to the principal of the school who often was not properly trained or not interested in providing professional development opportunities for teachers. Some teachers sought answers in higher-education programs, but if school districts would not help pay for the tuition costs, most teachers could not pursue an advanced degree on a teacher's salary.

The Effective Schooling movement began soon after the release of *A Nation at Risk* and at its heart was this premise: Find schools that are succeeding where many others fail, and document what these schools do. Then, set up a list of these things that other schools can duplicate to achieve similar results. One of the listed items was that school principals needed to be strong instructional leaders, with the charisma of Gandhi, the intimate knowledge of education of Bloom, and the compassion of Mother Teresa. Even if enough of these awesome individuals were around to fill the thousands of principal positions in America, the changes that new legislation mandated were coming at us with such velocity that no one school leader could possible do it all.

Nevertheless, there was still another problem in education that teachers knew about but were almost helpless in solving themselves. This problem was left out of *A Nation at Risk*, but was real as any of the problems it did explore. The profession of education had never reached its respected place in American society and American teachers had never been appreciated as true professionals. It might be because of a throwback to the days when teaching was "a woman's job" or "a second income job".

However, we believe that it was because teachers were not truly valued in terms of school leadership responsibilities. We never thought the day would come during our career when the decision-making authority would become a shared experience between administration and teaching staff, or that teachers would work in a school where a collaborative work culture among teachers would flourish.

Before *A Nation at Risk*, teachers mostly worked in isolation. One professor called it the "egg-carton environment". The school was the carton, the eggs inside were individual teachers, but careful Styrofoam barriers were constructed to prevent teachers from actually interacting with each other. It was the norm: teachers simply did not engage in professional collaboration. We have both witnessed teachers selfishly keeping their best teaching strategies to themselves as individuals in competition with the other to get a better evaluation or recognition from the principal. We say it was the poison that was at the heart of a failing education system. However, it was so ingrained in the system that it would be hard to modify, even though modifications were impossible to stop during this new era of educational change.

The real change agent that promoted teacher leadership was education's age of accountability. Along with the new standards, mandates, and testing programs came the notion that educators will be accountable for the performance of their students. Revolutionary at the time, it soon became reality for schools across the country. In addition, with the increased accountability, came the stress and anxiety of performance in this new educational model set forth by state and national mandates. The result was that teachers started to turn to one another to seek answers to the educational problems they faced and the age of teacher collaboration was officially born.

Twenty years into the change process, we work in an environment of a collaborative work culture, shared learning communities, job-embedded professional dialog and feedback, and colleague supporting colleague as we work through the climate of school improvement. Moreover, it is in this climate peer-coaching models have evolved to formalize the collaborative process that is growing in schools today.

In addition, when the National Commission on Teaching & America's Future published their latest report called: "What Matter's Most: Teaching for America's Future", the report concentrated on teachers as the heart of what determines success in student performance. The report says that curriculum, standards, resources, assessments, methodologies, and reforms do not have much impact on student achievement unless teachers have appropriate access to knowledge, collegial interaction, role models, continuous professional development and learning opportunities. However, teachers need support to embrace the challenges of 21st century teaching and learning. Rogers (1995) reveals the following to summarize this fact as he believes educators go through stages to adopt new innovations. The stages are:

1. Knowledge - when the person or group begins to learn and know about a new innovation
2. Persuasion - the person begins to form attitudes through interactions with others
3. Decision - there is a drive to seek additional information and a decision is made
4. Implementation - as regular use is attempted more information is sought
5. Confirmation - Continued use is justified or rejected based on the evidence of benefits or drawbacks.

Teacher interaction is the key to the success of 21st century learning to support each other and our students. Thus, we have entered the age of digital tools and peer coaching. Technology peer coaching is a support model that empowers teachers to collaborate with each other as they embrace changes. Peer into our thoughts in each chapter as we explain why we believe this professional development model meets 21st century teacher needs.

-Chapter 1-

What is Technology Peer Coaching?

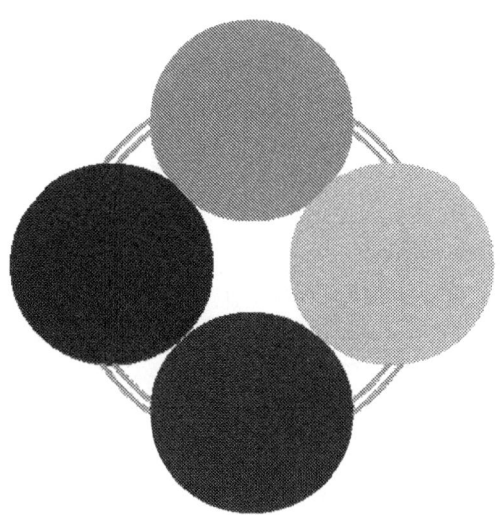

Technology Peer Coaching is a professional development model that is aligned with the *process* and *context* National Staff Development Council Standards. Times have changed, students have changed, learning has changed, and teachers are challenged in every way to keep up with the demands of the 21st century. With that being said, if we want teachers to keep up with the demands of the 21st century, they need support to implement new strategies in the classroom. The partnership for 21st century teaching and learning reveals that students learn differently and need to know different skills to survive in today's society. The strategies and skills that are required to provide a world class education for students has to be gained through professional development and is no doubt the key for all stakeholders. However, *effective* professional development is needed to do so.

The North Central Research Education Lab (NCREL) has identified characteristics for effective professional development that include:

- Learning community time during the teacher's workday to provide training, practice, and follow-up support
- A collaborative work culture
- Inquiry-based approach to teaching and learning
- Multiple avenues for collaboration with colleagues
- Reinvention of teacher professional development
- Overhaul of teacher recruitment to put effective teachers in schools
- Encourage and acknowledge teaching knowledge and skill

The answer to implementing all of these suggestions is Technology Peer Coaching. We have found that peer coaching is effective in helping teacher's impact instruction through the use of digital tools with students. As Technology Peer Coaching strategies are implemented, teachers begin designing lessons where students are able to accomplish tasks they would not able to do without digital tools and resources.

Technology Peer Coaching improves not only existing teaching practices, but is also the best way to introduce new teaching practices; is not the "one-shot" workshop that lacks follow-up and continued support; and is a lifestyle for teachers in schools who have adopted its use. So, then, what exactly is Technology Peer Coaching? It is the same process, but teachers are shown how digital tools and resources can be seamlessly integrated into the curriculum. Two or more professional colleagues still work together for a specific, predetermined purpose in order that teaching performance may be improved as well as validated (Becker, 2005). That purpose is to enhance student achievement through engaging technology integrated lessons. The assumption is if professional practice is to be improved, and thus student learning improved, teachers need accessible opportunities to share ideas, collaborate, reflect on their practice, and ask for assistance when necessary. In this way, we encourage successful teachers and successful teaching results in successful students. There are many peer-coaching models, and we will explore them in subsequent chapters, but essentially, they all have the same goal: improvement of student learning.

Peer coaching is based on research. Here is a summary of it:

- **5%** of learners will transfer a new skill into their practice as a result of theory
- **10%** will transfer a new skill into their practice with theory and demonstration

- **20%** will transfer a new skill into their practice with theory, demonstration and practice with training
- **25%** will transfer a new skill into their practice with theory and demonstration, practice with training, and feedback
- *90%* will transfer a new skill into their practice with theory and demonstration, practice with training, feedback, and coaching. (Joyce, 1987)

Technology Peer Coaching is the most effective professional development strategy to impact instruction through the use of digital tools and resources. The author's call it the technology integration game (TIG©) where teachers use peer coaching strategies to engage all students in learning. The peer coaching cycle and the implementation process is similar to preparing for student instruction. Teachers are empowered to assess, set goals, prepare, implement activities, and reflect/debrief. As teachers realize that this professional development model is aligned very closely with the teaching and learning cycle, the light bulb goes on that technology integration is not separate. The individual must decide that it is important to align the curriculum with the appropriate tools students can use to complete the activities or projects.

All teachers want to be the best teachers they can be, and want their students to be the best students they can be. One of the goals of the No

Child Left Behind legislation is that all students and teachers must have been technology literate by December 2006. Our district worked hard to meet the goal, but still found that most teachers were not engaging students with digital tools. We quickly found that literacy and integrating technology had a different meaning. We also found that professional development is the only way to help teachers accomplish this mission as many were not taught this way in the 20th century. In addition, teachers are coming to teaching as a second career and may know how to use technology tools; but not integrate it into the curriculum to engage students. Technology advocates are still striving to find effective ways to help teachers do so as the educational arena is the appropriate place to teach kids how to use digital tools and resources safely and appropriately.

When peer coaching came along, we quickly found that it was the resource to build the human infrastructure support needed to play the TIG, impact instruction and win the learning game. The TIG is a metaphorical concept where school teams which include administrators and teachers envision themselves as a team of players who engage students with digital tools to win the learning game. Students begin by taking assessments at home plate to drive instruction. Teachers design and deliver lessons through project based learning to engage students at first, second, and third base. Afterwards, they reflect and debrief on the outcomes of the project to determine if students achieved the lesson objectives. The students who create outstanding projects earn homeruns and are elected to play in outfield positions as student technology coaches. We are excited that the peer coaching program formalizes this process as teachers begin to learn strategies from each other to play the technology integration game.

Our experience with teachers has been that many feel unqualified in the area of technology, but the ones that do have something to offer their colleagues. Technology Peer Coaching is a model that recommends schools to provide teachers the opportunity to collaborate, exchange ideas, establish a connection with other teachers, engage in professional dialogue and establish a common language to help integrate technology tools and resources that our students already gravitate towards. Peer coaching becomes a "win-win" situation for both the technology peer coach and collaborating teacher.

The Technology Peer Coaching model was developed by the Puget Sound Center and funded through Microsoft in 2004. The model was built and designed on existing research by Joyce and Showers (1987). Technology Peer Coaching is designed to help teachers integrate technology, coach, and mentor a collaborating teacher to play the TIG© thereby engaging students. Working through the peer coaching process defined in the graphic below, helps teachers to continue reflecting/debriefing on all or parts of the cycle to improve the instructional game.

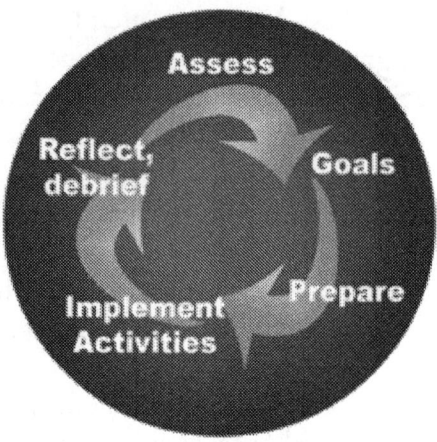

"Adapted from the *Peer Coaching* program, sponsored by Microsoft, and used with the permission of the Puget Sound Center for Teaching, Learning and Technology."

As teachers work through this process they begin to communicate and collaborate by working together learning how to engage students; thereby enhancing student achievement. The assumption is that the more teachers engage students, the more the students achieve. The peer coaching model is performance based as it requires actions at all levels to integrate the technology tools. The model reiterates the need for ongoing professional development where learning communities are developed empowering teachers to continue growing as a professional.

The reflection/debriefing part of the peer coaching model also helps teachers who want to assess how the new strategies are impacting instruction in the classroom. Teachers are challenged to use higher level thinking skills to improve teaching strategies just as athletes do to win a sports game. The technology peer coach uses a structured communication protocol to communicate through active listening, clarifying and paraphrasing what is heard, and the use of probing questions to help teachers determine new strategies to enhance instruction with technology. The communication protocol is used continuously until the teacher is comfortable coming up with strategies that are successful in the classroom.

To summarize this section, we have found that peer coaching is just like athletic coaching. Coaches determine the plays the teams will run time and time again. When the plays are not effective, coaches immediately reflect on new strategies needed to win the game. The players implement the new strategies in hopes of a productive outcome to lessen their losses. Athletes and coaches are challenged to use higher level thinking skills as they never know how well their opponent is prepared. The ultimate goal for teams of athletes is to become collaborative experts to win the game. Teachers must do the same to survive in the digital age of the 21st century. Students understand the game concept and educators can learn how to engage them in the TIG©. In the next chapter, we will explore the exciting benefits Technology Peer Coaching brings meeting the needs of 21st century teachers.

-Chapter 2-

Benefits of Technology Peer Coaching

Technology Peer Coaching benefits the entire school. The administrators, teachers and students all benefit in different ways. However, in order for any new teaching strategies to be successful for all concerned, they must be beneficial to all involved. Technology Peer Coaching is no exception. There is a direct correlation between the success of a peer coaching effort and the level of trust between the collaborating teachers. Teachers have to be aware of individual requirements so that the collaboration effort can be tailored to their needs. The peer coaching model involves teachers observing other teachers to know their strengths and weaknesses. The observation has to be done in a non-threatening, non-judgmental manner, and must involve a high degree of professional trust that insures that the peer coach is there to help, not criticize.

Through our experiences, the benefits of the peer coaching process are realized when professionals can enter into a non-threatening collaborative experience that involves teaching and learning new innovative strategies that are based on research and best practices. Some of the benefits reported by professionals who have been involved in peer coaching are:

- Improved student achievement
- Enhanced student progress
- Enhanced sense of professional skills

- Increased ability to analyze their own lessons
- Better understanding of what we know about best practices in teaching and learning
- A wider repertoire of instructional strategies/resources
- Deeper sense of efficacy
- Stronger professional ties with colleagues
- Improved teaching performance
- A better articulated curriculum
- More cohesive school culture
- Positive school climate

(Becker, 2007)

Benefits for Veteran Teachers

America's teachers today are older, better educated, and have more experience than ever before, according to a study released by the National Education Association. The study, based on information provided by a sample of the nation's 2.5 million schoolteachers, says that almost 67 percent of the country's public schoolteachers are over the age of 40, 54 percent have their master's degree or at least six years of college, and 38 percent have been teaching more than 20 years, with the mean a hefty 16 years (Surpuriya & Jordan, 1997). Veteran teachers have been playing the traditional teaching game well, as most are digital immigrants. A plus to this group is that they usually know their content area and may only need a little coaching to play the TIG©.

When the majority of these teachers entered the profession, computers in the classroom were an exception rather than the rule. All of the innovations that have spawned from an Internet connection were not even a dream 16+ years ago. The changes in technology have come quickly and furiously. Many veteran teachers are not technology literate, either because they have resisted change, or just have not had the professional development opportunities. Now many of these teachers feel so far "out of the loop" that they fear they will never catch up to their colleagues. As a result, teachers learn only what they absolutely "have" to do with the computer on their desk (i.e. putting grades into a grade book) or answering e-mails and continue to teach with the strategies used for two decades.

There are two strikingly apparent dangers in updating veteran teachers with the latest technology skills. First, the students we teach are not anything like the students of twenty years ago. Second, students enter school today as multi-tasking, visual, multi-media learners who come with technology skills that teachers have yet to learn. If teachers try to instruct these students using the technology they feel most comfortable with, i.e. VCR and overhead projectors, they will notice a great decrease in an already short attention span and very little learning taking place. The key is to get teachers involved in the technology integration game in which they learn how to engage students with the tools they are using in this digital age. As most of you know, students want to learn in an interactive environment that employs video, audio, animation, and specific and frequent individual response. The bottom-line is students want to be an active part of the learning process. Without the use of today's newest technology tools, teachers and students may feel frustration and failure.

There is still more work to be done as teachers who do use technology and authentic assessment projects in their classrooms are not preparing students to succeed in today's world. The Information Age has required that employable individuals have technology literacy skills such as researching Internet data, word processing, spreadsheet and database skills, and working successfully with teams on specific projects where multimedia reporting is essential.

Veteran teachers who have taken the risk and entered the game using the technology peer-coaching strategies have reported not only the benefits previously mentioned, but also:

- An increased appreciation for reflective practice
- A sense of more effectiveness as a teacher
- A new perspective on their profession
- A renewal of their own commitment to teaching

The benefits of Technology Peer Coaching for the veteran teacher may be the answer to "teacher burnout", which many experience in the profession. In addition, if the stress of teaching can be turned into the excitement that games do for students, perhaps we will retain more of our experienced teachers in the classroom for longer than the minimum retirement age. That would be a "win-win" situation for our schools, our students, and our country.

Benefits to New and Alternative Certification Teachers

It is no longer a prediction: there is a true teacher shortage in America. Top professionals are leaving for new and more lucrative careers, and fewer college students are opting for an education degree. Some states, like Florida and California, are experiencing greater student enrollments and with state mandates of smaller class sizes, school boards are hiring more out of field teachers to fill classroom spots. Out-of-field teachers are individuals who have a college degree in ANYTHING and can pass the scrutiny of the background screening to make sure they are not a convicted felon, and express an interest in wanting to teach school. These teachers are given a few years to pick up education classes in the evenings, and with no internship – no real preparation at all – they are put in front of students with a textbook in one hand and a set of state standards to be taught in the other. We teach in a large Florida school district that hired more than 1100 new teachers in 2006. Sixty percent of those teachers participated in the alternative education teacher program and we are expecting an even greater percentage this year. Some of these teachers have computer application skills. Some have none. Even the ones who can use word processing or email have no clue how to integrate what they know into what they teach.

The benefits of Technology Peer Coaching and playing the TIG© are evident. Not only will these teachers learn the use of technology in the classroom, but the residual effects of working with an experienced teacher will help direct the Alternative Certified teacher into using the best practices and research-based strategies, that work in the classroom.

Building a strong collaborative community with veteran teachers will bring the new teacher a sense of non-threatening collegial sharing. Even the teacher who comes into the profession from a standard teacher-education program will need help with the technology and integration techniques available that others have found both powerful and workable at the school. The benefits unique to this group are:

- Learning the best practices, strategies, and methods from experienced teachers
- Teaching long-term classroom teachers some of the latest innovations they may have encountered in the workplace or college degree programs that may translate into workable strategies at school.

- Building a community of trust with a peer group of teachers who trust, help, and support each other.
- Having a non-judgmental team member to ask if help is needed.

Benefits for the Technology Peer Coach

Before participating in a Technology Peer Coaching program we were both avid technology users and used cutting-edge technology in day-to-day lessons. The strategies were powerful and students, as well as teachers responded quickly, learned more, and were more motivated. We thought our successes were in application of integrated technology, but the applications are not nearly as powerful as it is when technology is integrated across a subject area, a grade level, or an entire school. When you have a group of teachers where students are using technology tools to engage in learning, we have witnessed that student learning increases exponentially, discipline problems decrease, and teachers learn new strategies from each other everyday. Teacher leadership qualities become apparent and opportunities for professional growth abound. An atmosphere of sustained peer-support from day-to-day makes everyone's job easier. Specific benefits of providing technology peer coaches to other teachers are:

- Technology peer coaches are empowered to share their knowledge with others
- Formalized collaboration between teachers who are technology savvy and those who want to learn to play the technology integration game
- More reflection on the peer coach's teaching strategies
- A better collaborative atmosphere among all teachers

Benefits of Playing the Game as an Administrator

For a peer-coaching program to succeed, administrative support is vital. So, why would a school administrator want to provide resources to a program such as peer coaching? It is simple. The initiative fosters a way for teachers to increase technology skills and engage students in the technology integration game. Teachers learn how to design lessons where students use the technology to enhance student achievement. Research proves it and practice makes it possible. However, improved student learning is not the only reason so many administrators endorse the peer-coaching models. Specifically, administrators have found that peer coaching:

- Utilizes school leaders to their greatest capacity

- Fosters a collaborative environment among teachers
- Provides job-embedded, supportive, and ongoing professional development opportunities for teachers
- Is cost-effective
- Empowers collaborating teachers to play the technology integration game with students

Benefits of Peer Coaching for Students

Finally, but most importantly, peer coaching has meaningful benefits for students. Peer coaching teams instill the use of cutting-edge strategies into the learning process. Below are additional ways students are impacted by peer coaching:

- Students become active, participatory learners
- Uses organization skills (CRISS strategies)
- Participates in an alternative learning style
- Are assessed through authentic means
- Performs authentic tasks (Life skills)
- Participates in peer coaching activities
- Collaborates on projects and works collegially (KAGAN strategies)

- Uses higher-level thinking levels in evaluation, application, and synthesis of ideas
- Achieves content achievement at an engagement level much higher than report writing
- Student becomes a communicator of knowledge to others
- Student becomes a designer of effective and stimulating communication
- Student masters research skills and information seeking strategies
- Utilizes inquiry-based learning
- Participates in instructional change
- Integrates technology into curriculum projects
- Participates in peer review
- Uses authentic project-based outcomes to share their work
- Utilizes reflection in a way which improves their skills
- Participates in planning, writing, and narrating projects which promotes reading literacy in its truest format

Therefore, all parties involved in establishing and maintaining a peer-coaching team feel good about their involvement. Teachers like the benefits they receive and are invigorated by the new strategies they learn, new resources they acquire, new projects they can introduce to their students, and, perhaps most importantly, the opportunity for reflection on the results of playing the TIG©. The Technology Peer Coaching program may begin as a way to better integrate technology into the curriculum, but its benefits reach farther than the use of technology alone. The benefits of the program touch the heart and soul of the profession itself and can be implemented by any teacher regardless of their content area expertise.

In the next chapter, let's look at how implementation of a Technology Peer Coaching program meets the needs of 21st century teachers.

-Chapter 3-

Implementing Technology Peer Coaching

Technology Peer Coaching is a 21st century professional development model that provides educators with strategies to win the technology integration game. Metaphorically, the players can be viewed as a sports team with a head coach (administrator), assistant coaches (assistant principals), and major league players (technology-savvy coaches) who mentor aspiring major league players (collaborating teachers) to improve their technology integration game. The graphic below reveals metaphorically how 21st century teaching and learning is like playing baseball. Everyone is engaged as a team just as baseball players to win the game.

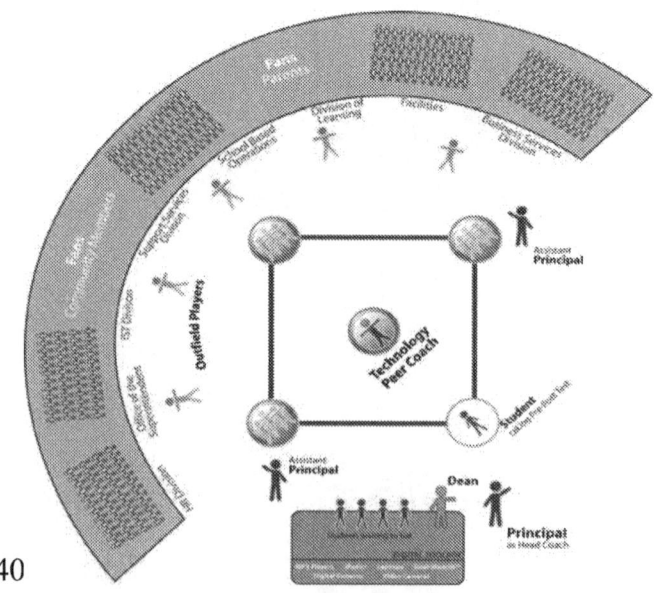

The purpose of the Technology Peer Coaching Program is to provide teachers with learning experiences that will further their professional skills and provide enhanced instruction for their students. We have found that as major league players, technology coaches work with collaborating teachers (aspiring major league players), to play the technology integration game. The goal is to empower aspiring major league players to eventually take on the role of a coach. The cycle helps teachers to integrate technology with student's one classroom at a time, thus building collaborative learning communities instead of working in isolation. As most of us know, isolation is the game educators have played in the past.

Unlike most educational attempts at professional development, Technology Peer Coaching has certain qualities that must be in place in order for this strategy to succeed. Technology peer coaches are the human infrastructure support systems needed to empower each other. Technology peer coaches can go beyond building a knowledge base and understand the needs of teachers that want to use technology in the classroom. During the coaching relationship, collaborating teachers as aspiring major league players focus instead on actually using the new knowledge base in daily teaching. Peer coaching also empowers teachers to re-design lessons to implement projects with students. This emphasis can be rewarding for the individual teacher, the school environment itself, and ultimately for the students affected by the system.

The technique of utilizing Technology Peer Coaching to integrate technology throughout the curriculum is dependant on several key principles:

- Teachers involved in the program must "buy-in" to the concept of peer coaching.
- Time must be provided for teachers to do collegial observations and engage in mutual feedback and evaluation.
- Administrative support for the process must be present.
- The process needs to be incorporated into the school's mission and/or school improvement plan.
- There must be a general understanding by all teachers and administrators that the process will change the school climate somewhat and that, while change is uncomfortable, it is necessary to stimulate professional growth.
- All faculty & staff must understand that the ultimate purpose of peer coaching is to provide improved learning opportunities for students.

Let's look at each of the above points in detail and explore how Technology Peer Coaching can help aspiring major league players play the technology integration game.

Teacher "Buy-In"

Teacher buy-in must be sought before pairing them with another colleague to learn technology integration strategies. As we look at the way the game was played in the past by teachers and students, schools functioned in what our friends termed "an egg-carton existence." Like a Styrofoam egg carton, teachers were grouped together in the same building, but they were insulated from each other and rarely touched each other's sacred domain—much like eggs in a carton that never touch each other. The norm was that each of us went into our classrooms every day and taught children in the best manner we could, never intruding on the sanctity of another teacher's territory. Instead of sharing effective strategies teachers isolated themselves in order to gain a competitive edge over other teachers. We have often wondered if competition between teachers was a result of the evaluation process used at schools or if the profession was simply steeped in loneliness and isolation. In either case, competition was not something that college had prepared us for and we have wondered if others felt the same?

The *Nation at Risk* report published in the 1980's criticized the American education system.

We believe this report alone caused teachers to realize that our biggest resource for changing the system was each other—and that together we had the answers to the problems we faced. The culture of educational collaboration began. Technology Peer Coaching is a formalization of this collaboration process.

We have also found that buy-in from teachers is much easier, because many want to know how to use 21st Century digital tools. Teachers want to learn new technologies, but many times, sticking with the same lesson plan is much easier. Through the implementation of Technology Peer Coaching, our experience has been that the use of technology tools in the classroom has empowered teachers.

Aspiring major league players are encouraged by the fact that the technology coaching model helps them to learn and implement a shared vision, a means of adding new knowledge to a teacher's repertoire, a demonstration and model of the skill in practice, and a reflection of how successful the practice was in real-life application. No matter which model of peer coaching you choose to implement in reading, technology, math or any other content area, success is dependent upon teacher buy-in. Aspiring major league players have an opportunity to realize that by working together we can share knowledge. Communicating our know-how also provides an enhanced learning experience for our students. When individuals are empowered to try new tools to enhance teaching, the results often lure others into the game.

Adequate Time

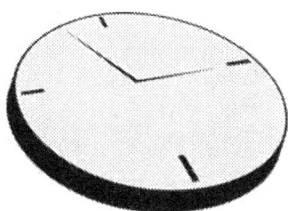

Adequate time is important if educators want to re-invent the delivery of instruction in the classroom. Technology can certainly help with the task, but we have found designing lessons often takes more time when teachers begin using technology. We have found aligning the curriculum with technology tools requires more time planning on the front end before implementation. Students, however, tell us that most of the time instruction is more effective when using some form of technology to accomplish the objectives. Stakeholders must understand that schools are not composed of buildings and institutionalized procedures, but with dedicated individuals who want to devise methods to improve education according to the needs of our modern society. Technology Peer Coaching is a model that encourages the use of structured time for educators to engage in meaningful collaboration to accomplish these objectives.

Structured release time provides the environment for these activities to take place, but also accomplishes an even more important function. During the structured time the basis for personal interaction and communication can lead to a climate of trust between the educational professionals. Without this foundation of trust, any attempt at systematic change will not succeed. By working together, solutions to problems can be found that are integrated and continuous.

Clearly, investment in release time at least monthly throughout the school year for aspiring major league players will pay dividends worth much more than money. Investing in this time will also help define the roles that educators are willing to take in a change process that is needed to provide better student instruction.

Administrator support

This component of successful Technology Peer Coaching implementation is very important and an entire chapter of this book is devoted to it. So, at this point, know that visionary administrative leadership that is willing to take risks and facilitates change rather than directs it is indispensable to the task. Without it, all efforts to use Technology Peer Coaching to integrate technology across the curriculum are doomed from the start.

Alignment of School Improvement Plan with Peer Coaching

Most institutions are guided by written statements that delineate the organization's mission statement, goals, objectives, and plan to accomplish these goals and objectives. In most schools, guiding entities set the agenda for progress at that school site. They take the form of School Advisory Councils comprised of teachers, administrators, parents, and community leaders who all have a stake in the success of the school to provide the best possible education to its students. In addition, the document created by the council takes the form of a School Improvement Plan. Different locations call this committee and the document it creates by different names, but the premise of its existence remains essentially the same.

By this measure, Technology Peer Coaching becomes part of the vision—the mission of the school. The goals of the Technology Peer Coaching initiatives are written complete with measurable objectives and supporting initiatives that will enable the school to reach their objectives. Most importantly, as part of the school's official improvement plan, use of the school's budget to support the effort is definable and accessible. Implementation steps begin and individuals responsible for their realization are chosen.

Best of all, the Technology Peer Coaching effort takes on an enhanced role in providing better education for the students. Validity and weight is there and changes from a strategy to a plan, and technology coaches and collaborating teachers feel more inclined to be a part of this important collaboration and team.

After implementation, the goals, objectives, strategies, and assessment and evaluation methods are used to judge the success of the program. Assessment of the program is an important step in the process of school progress that should not be ignored.

Stimulating Professional Growth

Teachers have historically been the final link in the chain of the hierarchy when change occurs in the school. District personnel, site administrators, or worst of all - outside consultants, decide what needs to be done and how it will be accomplished. Often times, teachers have little or no input into the process or the product leaving them feeling as if they are just another cog in the wheel of institutionalized education. No wonder they have been so resistant to the thought of new changes— even if those changes are vital for the students.

With Technology Peer Coaching, the hierarchical order is turned upside down. Major league players become the principal change agents in the school setting. Often, for the first time in their careers, they are asked for their collaborative opinions on how to improve instruction utilizing technology and are empowered to make changes. While some aspiring major league teachers are intimidated by this change, most feel elated and delighted with the opportunity to create new procedures. We have come a long way from the egg carton schools of the past, as we believe Technology Peer Coaching to be the crowning achievement in the quest for technology integration and 21st century student education.

Unfortunately not everyone will hop on the Technology Peer Coaching bandwagon. Change does not come easily for some individuals, and the process at times, can create uncomfortable and sometimes unpleasant situations even for those who *want* to change. Technology Peer Coaches and collaborating teachers need to be forewarned that there will be unavoidable – but manageable- bumps in the road. All change brings personal concern, but if the objective of more effective student performance is always kept at the forefront, personal concerns will not be able to impede success. If we expect problems, they will not shatter our dreams when they do materialize. If everyone joins the team and stimulates professional growth, we will engage students in the classroom with the tools in which they are already familiar.

Enhancing Student Achievement through 21st Century Tools

Research shows that, in the past, as little as 10% of traditional in-serviced teaching strategies actually translated into classroom implementation. Rates of transfer were even low for teachers who volunteered for more training. As a result, some well-designed teaching models did not find their way into general practice and therefore had no effect or influence on the student learning environment (Showers & Joyce, 1996).

Existing peer coaching models operate on the premise that if teachers were given regular exposure to new strategies, time to implement the new strategies, support from experienced coaches, and time to reflect, the new strategies would become part of the teacher's regular practice and thus directly affect student learning. Research has proven that this technique translates into almost 90% implementation on a regular basis and as teachers create better learning environments for themselves, students learn more.

Efforts must be consciously made to keep the ultimate goal of improved student performance at the forefront. The curriculum and teaching must be the focus; the method must be secondary. Even if teachers do not use technology, the peer coaching model is designed to enhance student achievement. However, with technology integration, as the

Technology Peer Coaching program develops, teachers begin to accept that this new means to a better end is acceptable. We gently begin to win the technology integration game as we understand that technology is not separate, but should be seamlessly integrated into the curriculum when appropriate. Students of the 21st century are digital natives who will provide few challenges to use technology tools to accomplish curriculum goals.

      Student achievement is also enhanced when they are engaged. Teams are formed between students and teachers as we learn from each other, and from our mistakes just like athletic teams. We learn by sharing our collective knowledge, and by being risk-takers we learn by doing. We add a new dimension to our job as teachers and we improve instruction for students. In the next chapter, let's see why technology peer coaching works.

-Chapter 4-

Why does Technology Peer Coaching Work?

What makes peer coaching the most successful method of integrating technology throughout the curriculum? The answer to this question has several factors that work together in concert to make this professional development strategy superior to all others when looking at utilizing technology in the classroom. These factors include:

- Student needs
- Teacher needs
- Authentic assessment
- Technology integration mandates
- Reflection

Student Needs

Students in this age of information are visual, active, multi-sensory, multi-tasking, hands-on learners. If you have ever observed today's teenager doing a homework assignment, and you are over the age of 25, you marvel that they actually finish assignments at all. I have seen teenagers who can simultaneously use the computer to write an essay, have 2 or 3 chat windows open and know what conversations they are engaging in, have a cell phone in hand, an iPod in ear, MTV on the television in the same room, and eating a sandwich. As adults, we would probably be on sensory overload and our brain would shut down.

However, teenagers and young adults have grown up in a world that has always been audio-visual fantasylands and their brains have been conditioned to accept stimuli from various sources simultaneously. They are products of a technical age that learned the alphabet from Big Bird and watch more hours of television in a week than they are in school. Because of the Internet, they have access to resources that most of us never knew existed when we were that age. They can access primary source materials that only a few years ago were locked up in collegiate libraries and available only to doctorial candidates. They can look up every point of view on any subject and document them accordingly.

It is no longer important to know information—but more important to know how to find the information you need when you need it. The Information Age student has seriously challenged the traditional classroom environment. No longer can we expect them to stay on task for a 50-minute lecture. They simply will not be dazzled by overhead projection—no matter how intricate your overhead slides are! Our students today demand more interactive, visual, and challenging material. And if you feel ill equipped to provide it you are not alone.

Teacher Needs

Teachers are divided on the need for integrated technology in the classroom. There are those who are full of hope—and those who are full of fear. Let us look at each of these and their individual needs.

Hopeful Teachers

As intimidating as the change process can be, these teachers have embraced expanded use of technology in their classrooms. Most of them credit computers for greater student motivation and for more self-directed learning taking place. Technology provides hands-on skill building for abilities students will need in the 21st century. The Chinese proverb that says "Give a man a fish and he will eat; teach a man to fish and he will eat for a lifetime" applies to technology. Spoon-feed student information and he will learn; teach a student the means of finding information he needs, and he will learn for a lifetime. 21st century education sets the stage for life-long learning habits that experts say will be key to success in the future.

The use of technology enhances higher-level thinking. It takes learning to a global level, and brings resources into student hands that were never available before. There is a built-in excitement found in using technology that is absent from books.

Students gain a feeling of empowerment by finding information, and synthesizing it into presentations and other products that give them voice to enter into a dialog about their learning. It also creates a stage where they can examine problems and suggest solutions. Best of all, it allows teachers to work smarter—not harder. It enhances collaboration between students, teachers, and other educational professionals. It provides better instruction.

Fearful Teachers

These teachers have misgivings about the use of technology in schools. They feel that they may lose personal connection with their students—some even fear being replaced by computers. They feel a loss of self-confidence because they lack the technical skills in which many of their students excel. They sometimes feel they will lose control over material being taught in this age of state standards and teacher accountability. They fear they will be looked upon as incompetent. Those 20-year-old laminated lesson plans will be obsolete, and they panic at the thought that we expect them to change the entire way they have taught—when in reality we expect technology to enhance the way they teach. Then, there are those who simply fear the unknown.

    Teachers who are more pragmatic look at the thousands of dollars being spent on technology in schools today and worry if student achievement will suffer. They need not worry – research shows technology use has a positive impact on student achievement. Some cite technical problems with equipment that translates into loss of class time. Most fearful teachers feel they are just not prepared to teach with full technology integration. Even new teachers have voiced concerned that pre-service teacher education has not prepared them for the challenge.

    The reality of the situation is this: technology tools will never take the place of the teacher. It will only make the content you teach more accessible, reliable, and interesting. Students will still need the teacher to guide, monitor, correct, and steer them in the process. Teachers will always be the pedagogic experts in the room—no computer can replace that function.

Hope will eventually overcome fear because techniques such as peer coaching will pull down the barriers we have set up. We will soon come together and allow students to engage in a forum where they are most comfortable, take ownership of their learning, and are more successful. Teachers, as a by-product, will also become more comfortable and enjoy more success. Thanks to peer coaching, we will one day wonder how we ever managed without technology tools in classrooms.

Authentic Assessment

An authentic assessment usually includes a task for students to perform and a rubric by which their performance will be evaluated. It differs from traditional assessment which takes the form of multiple-choice tests, fill-in-the-blanks, true-false, matching and the like that have been and remain so common in education. Teachers do not need to choose between traditional and authentic assessment, but rather need to have a mixture of the two to serve many different purposes.

Authentic assessment is based on the theory that we do not want our students just to "KNOW" content and repeat it back to us, but what we really want is for students to "USE" content and demonstrate the meaning of what they have been taught. Authentic assessment not only serves as an assessment tool, but a learning tool as well. A well-planned authentic assessment assignment will allow students freedom of choice to demonstrate their knowledge in different ways. Some of the most common methods associated with authentic assessment are posters, oral presentations enhanced with presentation software slides, videos, and websites.

Differentiated learning models call for assessment of students utilizing multiple-intelligence methods and technology certainly has entered the arena of enhancing multiple intelligences. Knowledge can be synthesized into visual, auditory, text, art forms, music, or models. Technology is the tool that students can use to express themselves clearly, with organization, and in a professional manner. It allows teachers to do more authentic assessing of students than they have ever had the capability of doing before. It is clearly a helpful instrument for this process.

Peer coaching exploits authentic assessment to the fullest and allows for personal creativity on the part of the teacher and student alike. It gives meaning to learning.

Technology Integration Mandates

Technology in schools is an expensive undertaking. Equipment that becomes outdated quickly, support personnel to keep that equipment operational, server storage, wireless and fast Internet access with enhanced bandwidth, and training for school professionals in its use, is costing our school districts millions of valuable dollars.

It is no wonder that every state, as well as the federal No Child Left Behind legislation, set goals for the full integration of technology across the curriculum at all levels of education. Some mandates have even set strict timetables for implementation of technology integration. It can be very intimidating for teachers who already may feel inadequate abut their own technology skills.

      While most educators believe that government mandates for the use of technology is a bad idea, we understand the reason for them. Money is so precious to us in education that none can be wasted. If mandates were not put in place, the possibility of the equipment and resources being unused or underused is great.

      One way to alleviate some alarm that these new mandates will affect our performance and evaluation as a highly qualified educator is to admit our deficiencies and take steps to correct them. Technology Peer Coaching is the best answer to this complicated problem. By entering into a peer-coaching situation, teachers will take part in professional dialog with others who have more experience with technology, and some who are novices as well. Teachers will realize that their strength will be in numbers. Numbers of teachers learning to teach with technology for the improvement of student learning will find success. Do not let the mandates scare you – they are attainable.

Reflection

Modern teaching does allow a great amount of time for teachers to reflect on what they do, how they do it, and how they could improve their practice. Yet, reflection has been a tenet of our profession and key to its development and improvement. Just as we contrive ways of assessing the progress of students, we need to find ways to assess our own performance as well. This is especially important when we utilize technology in our teaching practice. However, reflection does not happen automatically. It takes purposeful action to do effective reflection and written outcomes if change is to be accomplished.

In Technology Peer Coaching, the written models include pre-determined rubrics on which to evaluate progress and set questions to answer and discuss with others. Using this method, we share learned knowledge about the outcome of the coaching experience as well as the process itself. Reflection assures us that if mistakes were made, they will not be repeated. It allows us to improve our methods and implementation strategies. It allows us to celebrate our successes. It is vital to the process.

Technology Peer Coaching addresses student needs, teacher needs, authentic assessment, mandates for integrating technology, and reflection of progress. Any or all of these could be obstacles to technology integration, but when addressed through a peer-coaching model, these factors become less problematic and more manageable for teachers. In the next chapter, we will view the characteristics needed to be an effective technology peer coach.

-Chapter 5-

What Characteristics are needed to be a Technology Peer Coach?

Teachers must be prepared to integrate technology into their teaching strategies. Teachers who mentor collaborating teachers must have the necessary characteristics to be effective technology peer coaches. Peer coaching, just like athletic coaching, is more than just having the desirable technical skills to infuse technology usage into lesson plans or the game. Peer coaching goes beyond providing assistance to the needs of colleagues in technology integration. Technology peer or athletic coaches must be mentors in every sense of the word and for a pre-determined amount of time. So the question becomes: What are the characteristics that a mentor needs to be an effective technology peer coach? Here is a list of the qualities one should look for in a successful peer coach:

- Master teacher
- Team member
- Researcher
- Collaborator
- Extensively trained
- Commitment to professional growth and development
- Confident & compassionate resource provider

Let's look at each of these qualities in detail...

Peer coaches must be Master Teachers

Master teachers are those who create positive and high expectations for students. Master teachers have the capability to plan and carry out exemplary lesson plans that focus on student learning.

They are excellent disciplinarians. They should have a desire to present lessons, and follow-up on their implementation. They must also be able to engage in reflection on instructional methods and articulate the need for goals. Similarly, athletic coaches must be masters in their game while at the same time have the ability to empower others to become great players.

Peer coaches must be Team Players

Effective peer coaches must have a positive attitude toward their school, its policies, and their colleagues. They must be well liked by their peers, and held in high regard by their

administrators. They must have good interpersonal skills and demonstrate flexibility. Some coaches only help with planning, while others become true partners.

Those coaches who become true partners often team teach units with their collaborating teachers, and therefore, must embrace the concept of collegial sharing of methods and strategies that work in the classroom. Technology Peer Coaches are involved in every aspect of the team taught lessons (planning through assessment). Coaches help their collaborating teacher identify goals of the lesson, find resources, assist in the creation of the lesson plan, write assessments, and implement the activities. After the implementation of the lesson plan, the coach and the collaborating teacher debrief. Debriefing with the collaborating teacher following the unit is a good way to improve lessons taught and insures that students are provided authentic and stimulating activities.

Just like athletic coaches, peer coaches empower players to become true partners on teams. In most sports, a team effort is needed to win the game. In fact, even sports that focus on individual players involve some team effort between the player and the coach to move from good to great and survive the game.

Peer Coaches must be Researchers

Athletic coaches must research their opponent to determine strategies to win. If not, it is like going into a war unprepared. A great coach studies his opponent in great detail to empower his/her players with ammunition to win the game. Peer coaches must also research other professionals in order to obtain the skills and knowledge needed to support classroom technology usage. Research is a valuable resource for teachers who want to document their successful integration of technology in their lessons.

The coaching role requires the use of good communication skills such as paraphrasing and the frequent use of questions. These techniques ensure that the coach and the collaborating teacher are on the same page in their thinking. Using those skills, the coach evokes information from the teacher as to what the teacher needs to succeed and then supplies the teacher with the research, best practices, and curriculum design that aids in the connection of technology use to academic achievement.

Peer Coaches must be Collaborators

Collaboration cannot be mandated, it has to be a natural occurrence in the school. Collaboration involves assessing needs and resources, implementing new strategies, and debriefing and reflecting on results. Those activities involve commitment. Pressuring or forcing participants to commit to a peer-coaching program simply will not work. Only voluntary participation in a well-designed peer-coaching program will yield positive results. Voluntary participation is the only way both peer coaches and their collaborating teachers will be able to sustain the motivation and initiative needed to make a program successful. Athletic coaching involves the same collaborative efforts to determine which players are best for their team.

      Some athletic coaches study and follow players throughout their developmental years from youth league sports to high school to college leagues in order to determine if the players are a good fit for the team. In athletic coaching, coaching is a business, so they want the best players for their team. Collaborating with the coaches on the team helps ensure the right decisions. Empowering educators who want to become teacher leaders is the same concept as they can encourage, inspire, and motivate more teachers to turn good students into great students!

Peer coaches need Extensive Training

Peer coaches should be engaged in on-going professional growth, such as workshops, conferences, and graduate classes. They need to make sure they keep up with the latest educational technology innovations, and research. They must have a natural curiosity about engineering ways to use cutting-edge technology in the classroom. However, they must draw the line at the use of technology for technology's sake. Student education must be the basis of all lessons employing technology, and a good technology peer coach will know the difference between instructional technology tools that demonstrate student growth and technology used as an after-thought or add-on to a lesson plan.

Athletic coaching involves continuously providing practice from experts that can help their players improve from good to great. Training is not an option in athletic coaching. Training and practice is the most important thing athletes focus on other than winning the game. It is a business; and coaches know that in order for their players to improve, they must practice. Professional development must be similar so teachers have continued practice long after the training. As administrators empower teachers to integrate 21st century teaching skills, training is the key. Integration of technology is even better when there are teacher leaders on staff that can provide timely training.

Peer Coaches are committed to Professional Growth & Development

There is a huge difference between being knowledgeable about educational technology and actually using it as an integrated tool in the classroom. Peer coaches must have implemented the new strategies in real-life classroom situations before they begin to teach others about the implementation process. Professional growth and development is not measured by how many classes you take, seminars you have attended, or workshops you have completed. Perhaps the most important element of professional development comes from the actual implementation of the technology, the alterations one must make to make it workable in a given situation, and the reflection afterwards. It is with this knowledge that the peer coach can be most useful in their role. Just as a state license on the wall does not always make a good teacher, an impressive list of in-services and classes is not the only training needed by Technology Peer Coaches.

Most athletes are committed to professional growth as they know they will not remain on the team otherwise. Administrators must empower and challenge their teachers to grow professionally as well. Using the Individual Professional Growth Plan is a tool that can empower teachers to create a long term plan for professional growth to include ways project based learning can be implemented. Project based learning strategies provide the opportunity for students to interact and engage in learning using 21st century tools.

Peer coaches must have Confidence

Perhaps the most important quality in a successful peer coach is the human quality. Peer coaches need to have warm, caring, and inviting personalities and they must have the capacity to take a personal interest in their collaborating teacher. To do this, peer coaches must be sensitive to the needs of others.

There are several ways that coaches can show confidence and compassion. One way is for the coach to invite a collaborating teacher to observe a lesson, or the coach might teach a lesson in the collaborating teacher's classroom. Another way is to exhibit products of technology integration in hallways or the Media Center. Coaches could also regularly share student examples of technology projects at staff meetings. These types of activities will provide teachers new ideas and create opportunities to discuss ways of integrating technology. The peer coach must be flexible in his or her personal schedule to make the time necessary to engage others in mentoring technology skills.

Athletic coaches must be confident and compassionate or they will not survive societal pressures. Similarly, the peer coach must also show their teachers that they have confidence in the teachers. Peer coaches must also continue to empower collaborating teachers through the individual professional growth plan in order for the collaborating teacher to gain new knowledge and skills to keep up with the students in today's society.

Peer coaches must be Resource Providers

Technology Peer Coaches must be familiar with key hardware and software that is available for use, know how and where to search for resources, and provide directions & collaboration on technology use. Coaching is often an informal process that happens in a hallway or lunchroom where teachers discuss lessons they are doing or will do. Coaches can suggest technology that fits the lesson, Internet sites with valuable information, software available in the school, and can follow up with an e-mail to add to the discussion. These methods take advantage of the "teachable" moment to help collaborating teachers integrate technology. Therefore, peer coaches are outstanding teachers, thoughtful and caring people, expert technicians, and have the interpersonal skills necessary to convey knowledge, implement strategies, find resources, and reflect on outcomes. They provide the platform in which other teachers can access a learning opportunity that will allow them to further develop their professional skills.

Peer coaches provide opportunities for teachers to be observed and observe others. Successful peer coachers work in non-hierarchical environments in which they can learn as much as they teach others. Peer coaches provide feedback in the form of professional dialog, options to consider, and shared exploration of educational strategies. They do not judge, evaluate, or criticize. The peer coach and the collaborating teachers own all outcomes of the program. The ultimate winners of their efforts are the students who will be the recipients of instruction delivered using integrated technology. The main goal of peer coaching is student success. The goal is reached through professional partnerships and teamwork – things which are not always prevalent in educational institutions.

The record of peer coaching success has made it clear that this method works effectively in the schools that have used it. Research results also show that there will be a greater need for more good peer-coaches in coming years. Peer coaching is an element of the educational reform that has finally arrived to change us into 21st century schools. The future is now, and peer-coaching models will lead us through the complexity of integrating technology into traditional classrooms.

Administrators, like athletic coaches, must be resource providers. The team players will refer to them to offer guidance and resources. In addition, just as injuries occur in sports, setbacks can occur in the classroom. Coaches must be prepared and armed with the knowledge of how to assist their players and get them back in the game as soon as possible. Even though there may be other players, the stars are the ones who play in every game. Therefore, once a player has committed to the team, coaches cannot hire someone to take their place. When teachers commit to peer coaching, they need to realize that their commitment is serious. If we want teachers to integrate technology and enhance student achievement, training must be provided until it becomes a habit. A Chinese proverb summarizes peer coaching: "Tell me and I'll forget; show me and I may remember; involve me and I'll understand." In the next chapter, we will reveal how administrators can support technology peer coaching.

-Chapter 6-
Peer Coaching Models

"Adapted and used with the permission of the Puget Sound Center for Teaching, Learning and Technology."

There are many different models that can be implemented through Technology Peer Coaching. The models are similar to positions on athletic sports teams. However, Microsoft's Peer Coaching Program defines three models that have been implemented effectively as 1) Part time; 2) Grade level/Department Chair and 3) Media Specialist. From both of our experiences with peer coaching at the school level, the most widely used is the part time model.

To be successful, administrators and teachers must determine what models will work best for the school and identify key players. Schools may also decide to implement all three models. For visionaries that support technology integration, utilization of all three models will help develop a technology savvy staff within a few years.

All of the models require that the head coach (the administrator), and the key players (the teachers), be on the same page by planning and integrating the school support agreement into the school improvement /technology plan. At each school different models may be chosen to meet the needs of each school. However, peer coaching is unique in that it encourages the development of teacher leaders no matter what school implements the plan. Just as the part time model will work for some schools, the grade level department chair model may be good for others. Each model is unique and only works if it is appropriate for the school.

It does not matter which model the school implements, all models are designed to meet the same goals of increased student achievement, more engaged students, and technology integration into the curriculum. However, everyone must be in agreement or the implementation will not be as successful.

From the district and school level, we have experienced all three models implemented and have found that they all are effective. Success all depends on the administrator's goals and the support that he or she provides. Commitment to the program is fundamental to the program's success. The models do not make the program successful; they are only guides to provide options for schools to implement the plan. Now, let's explore the models in detail to understand them better.

The Part-Time Model

The part-time model is one where teachers have a full time teaching position, but has a desire to learn new technologies and mentor another teacher on technology integration. The teachers must find time to meet or if the school or district is supporting the program, funding may be provided for substitutes once a month or more if required so the teachers can work together. During this time, the part-time technology coach may assist by:

- Implementing lessons for the collaborating teacher to observe
- Planning for new lessons
- Assisting with the design of effective lessons
- Training on new equipment
- Setting up equipment
- Team teaching with the collaborating teacher during instruction time
- Reflecting and debriefing to make necessary adjustments in teaching practices

The research reveals that the most effective program provides the time for teachers to meet. This time provides the technology coach the time to meet the needs of the collaborating teacher. The strength of the coaching model rests in the communication, collaboration, and reflection to determine where improvements can be made while learning to implement new technologies.

Both teachers also learn from each other as one may be a more experienced content expert and the other may be technology savvy. The first goal is development of technology savvy teachers with content expertise! The ultimate goal is to win the game, or in our case, to increase student achievement.

As the research shows, teachers cannot make changes or implement anything new without the proper support. The support must be sustained and ongoing over an extended period of time. The sustained support allows the training to translate into classroom teaching practices. The table below reveals the benefits of ongoing, long-term support for teachers after training.

Type of Training	Knowledge Mastery	Skill Acquisition	Classroom Application
Theory +	85%	15%	5 - 10%
Practice +	85%	80%	10 - 15%
Coaching, Study Teams, Peer Visits	90%	90%	80 - 90%

This table was adapted from information found in Showers and Joyce's research on the impact of professional development.

The Grade-Level Model

The grade level or department chair model may be implemented in schools that focus on technology integration within school teams. This model works well for schools that want to quickly increase the number of teacher's integrating technology. The power in this model is that grade levels can be arranged to have the same planning time which allows them to work together collaboratively on a daily or weekly basis. Teachers using this model can also develop integrated thematic units across grade levels allowing students to use different technologies to complete projects. The flexibility, that is needed to work with teachers daily versus planned meeting times required for the part time or media specialist model, enables the grade level technology peer coach to locate resources, model, collaborate, or observe teachers as they integrate new lessons in the classroom. This is especially true if the grade levels have a common planning time and/or block scheduling.

From an athletic standpoint, all coaches plan time for the team to practice during common times because you cannot practice as a whole without all the members present. Technology coaching is no different and works much more efficiently when all parties are present at the same time, rather than when they are allotted the necessary collaboration time.

Even though this model can provide more benefits on a daily basis, the administrator must be involved to develop a plan that will work for the technology coach(s) and collaborating teachers. If the administrator is on board, it will be easier for any technology coach(s) to help teachers integrate technology or any other resource into the curriculum. The administrator must also be willing to find the funding that will help teachers obtain the tools necessary to integrate more technology in the classroom or the training will not translate into the classroom. Alternative funding is not an option if you want to move forward as schools will never have enough money.

We have observed and noted that schools who write numerous grants and participate in district grant opportunities are integrating more technology in the classroom. In a sense, administrators are collaborating with outside sources to fund technology equipment and stipends. Funding is an issue, but can be worked around by finding creative ways to implement your plan.

The Media Specialist Model

Like the pitcher on a baseball team, the media specialist model is very unique. The pitcher is the one that calls the plays and is connected to all the other players on the team. The media center is similar as it is the hub of the school and can serve as such for teachers that are interested in conducting research or need resources to implement projects. One benefit of this model is that Media Specialists can locate and provide many different types of resources for teachers. If the school has a flexible and open schedule for the media center, the Media Specialist can provide time to work with all teachers that are integrating technology into the curriculum.

For this model to be successful, the Media Specialist must also be on the school leadership or school improvement team. Through participation in this team, the Media Specialist can determine what curriculum resources teachers need to integrate technology effectively across all grade levels during instruction. Media Specialist with an open and flexible schedule can also assist teachers by working with students in the media center on units currently being studied in the classroom.

Another role the Media Specialist can portray with this model is of technology trainer. The Media Specialist can train teachers and other staff members on various technology resources or equipment before, during, and/or after school. Administrators that support the Media Specialist by providing the time required to assist teachers during the day with "just in time training" or support, enhances teaching and learning as teachers learn new strategies.

The bottom line is that all three models must be supported financially and each member should be a part of the technology team or school improvement team to help teachers get on board with technology integration. Teachers can also develop units in conjunction with the Media Specialist in which students will work on the project with both parties. The power of this model is incredible as all students in elementary grade levels are usually required to visit the media center during special block at least once a week.

Students have an advantage with this model because they can learn how to locate reliable and credible resources needed for their projects. Information literacy, copyright and ethics and technology literacy can be taught as well. This saves the teacher time during classroom instruction when both the Media Specialist and teacher collaborate together on the skills students will need to complete technology rich projects.

Schools that incorporate the Media Specialist model can direct funding in other ways as this position does not require a substitute teacher. If the school has an open and flexible media center and a media paraeducator, this model can be incorporated very effectively with little changes. Otherwise, funding must be provided for substitute days so both teachers have structured time to meet with each other.

The power in all three models is the collaborative efforts of teachers that result in project based learning activities with students. The TIG graphic is a glimpse of a collaborative effort by all stakeholders who support technology integration.

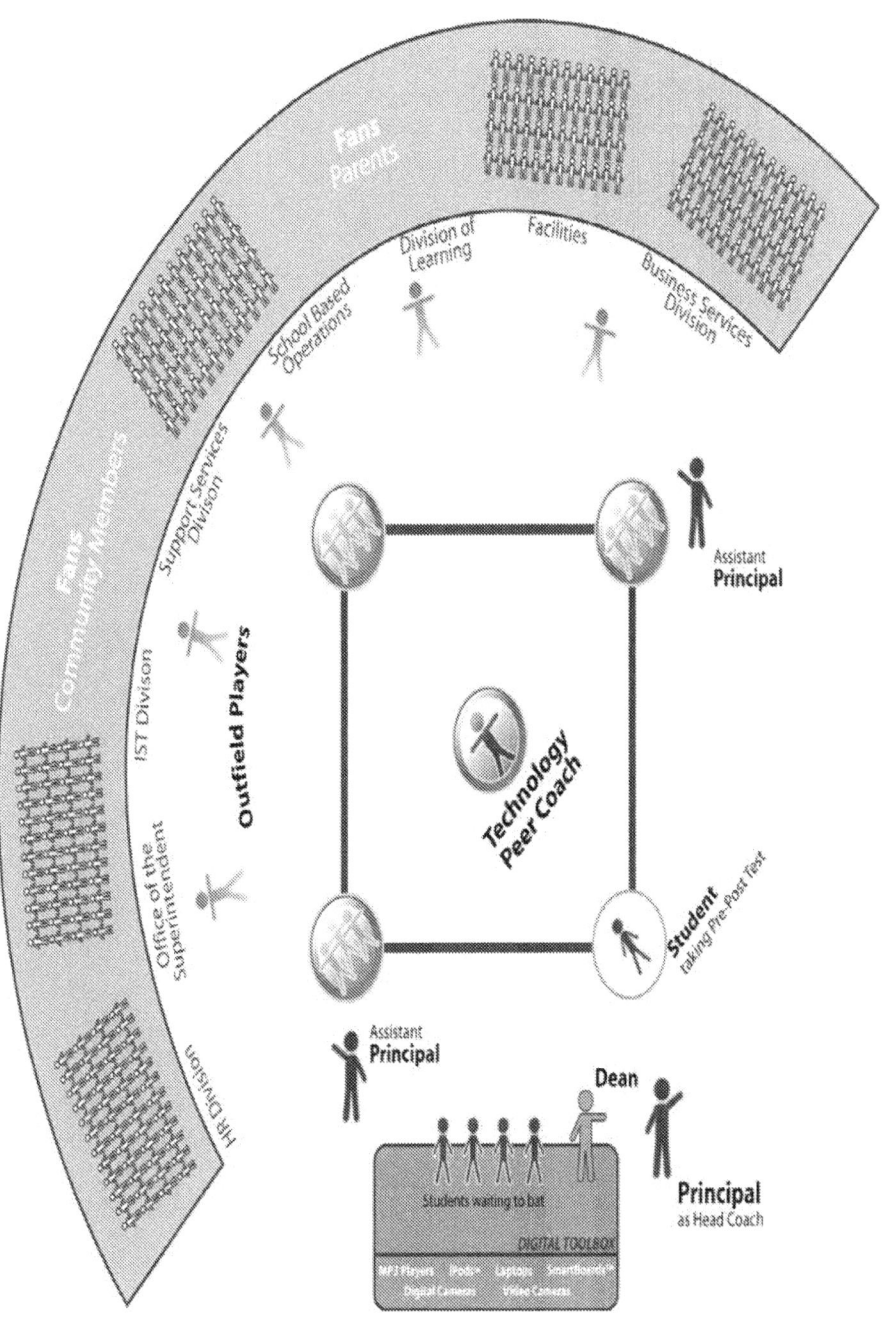

-Chapter 7-

Administrator Support

Administrator support is vital to the success of the technology peer coaching program. If you think of coaching in general, the head coach is the one that leads the team. Administrators can be thought of as the head coach of the peer coaching team. The technology peer coaches can be thought of as the pitcher that mentors collaborating teachers to take on this role of a coach with their students. The goal is to assist collaborating teachers to engage students in the classroom through the use of technology. To win teachers over, you must be able to show them how they will be supported while learning and integrating new technologies in the classroom. Collaboration or mentoring is critical to the development of technology skills for teachers and plays a role in improving student achievement. Administrators may find that learning how to coach new players through technology peer coaching can be challenging on one hand and exciting on the other. Robbins, 2007 says "determination alone is not enough to make changes; one must implement effective strategies to do so." Technology peer coaching teams must embrace a strong vision, commitment, and utilization of effective strategies to achieve the goal of a 21st century educators.

To support technology peer coaching, a plan must be in place and integrated with the goals related to student achievement or school improvement. Technology peer coaching can be aligned with any professional development model. The immediate benefit through this model is that teachers receive long term, ongoing, and sustained training. Peer coaching is aligned with two of the

National Staff Development Council Standards, Continuous Improvement Model and the Florida Professional Development Protocol Evaluation Standards. The graphic below reveals how the three models are interrelated.

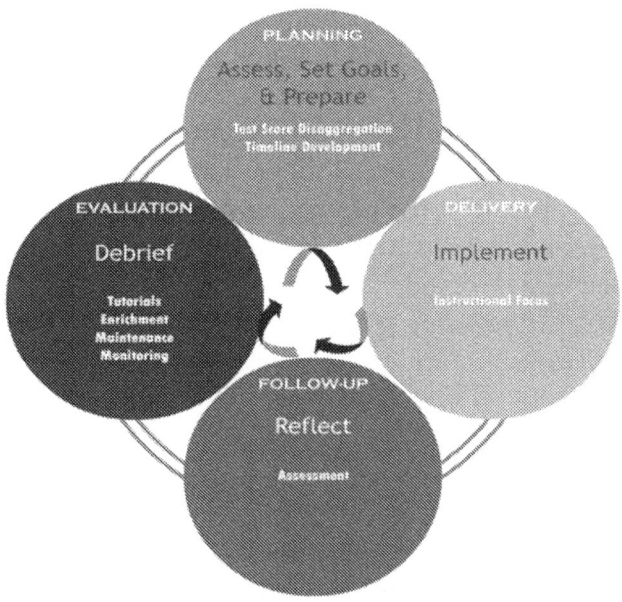

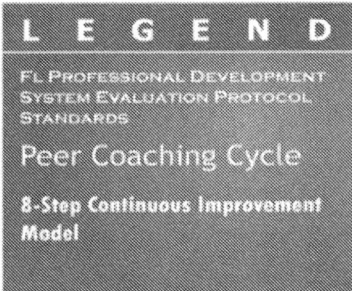

Now, let's see how administrators as head coaches can support and implement this model at the school level. Research supports building positive relationships and peer coaching does so through effective communication skills. In order to do so, administrators can use coaching skills identical to athletic coaches to seek out or develop key players to become teacher leaders. The peer coaching model stresses the development of teacher leaders that assess, set goals, plan, attend training, and collaborate with the collaborating teacher(s) to implement technology in the classroom. The model also reiterates reflection and debriefing an important part of the process that encourages continuous improvement. For those that want to implement the model, professional development must be attended to learn effective communication skills.

The communication skills are the backbone of the program as Covey (1997) says "Seek first to understand then be understood." Utilizing effective communication skills focuses the collaborating teacher on their needs as well as plans that are appropriate for them to integrate technology in the classroom. To obtain the training required to implement the program, schools can seek out assistance from their school district, local colleges, or Puget Sound Center for Teaching and Learning. Whichever model is chosen, administrators would be ahead of the game by remembering the following points to guide their school:

- Develop and share the vision for technology integration with staff members
- Integrate technology coaching into the school improvement/technology plan
- Provide structured time during the day for teachers to meet
- Attend professional development to stay abreast of technology integration
- Develop assessment instruments to assess and evaluate the impact of technology integration in classrooms
- Creative funding possibilities to provide new emerging technology tools for the classroom
- Schedule monthly meetings to adjust the goals of the program and determine how it is working

     Support involves more than the development of a school support agreement, vision, plan for technology integration and technology peer coaching. Once the Administrator shares the vision and planning has taken place, the technology leadership team must include technology peer coaches that collaborate frequently to develop and implement an action plan. Marketing is a great way to encourage teachers to join the team. The head coach as administrator will need funding assistance to implement the plan. We have found that grants and other creative funding avenues must be sought to implement the plan. We have also found that without funding for equipment and substitute time for teachers, the plan may not be as effective. Finding the appropriate funding to implement the plan in the following ways are recommended to support teachers:

- Purchase technology tools for both the technology peer coach and collaborating teacher
- Provide half day substitutes for the technology peer coach and collaborating teacher (at least 4-5 times during the year)
- Schedule and meet monthly to reflect/debrief on implementation with peer coaching team
- Assessment and evaluation instruments to determine outcomes

In short, due to a decrease in funding for technology in schools, administrators may find that creative funding is another avenue to help implement the plan. Administrators may find support through partnerships with the instructional or technology divisions in the district office.

Administrator support also involves collaboration and building collegiality with technology peer coaches and collaborating teachers. This ensures the success of the program and problems can be solved immediately to keep everyone on target while playing the game. Technology peer coaching is not an easy game. The administrator as head coach is the key to keep technology coaches and collaborating teachers excited about winning the game. The administrator must continue to meet frequently with the players, observe players as they practice in the classroom, and review the game plan to keep everyone on target. Visiting and observing players on each team are a must as teachers must know they are supported when engaging in a new game. Research conducted by David Collins in *Achieving Your Vision of Professional Development* reveals that collaboration and collegiality provide moral support for teachers who are experimenting with new strategies or participating in substantial reform projects.

Administrators must model what they expect of their team players and that includes building collaboration and collegiality amongst the entire team. Administrators can foster collaboration and engage staff members by:

- Leading by example
- Participating in projects with students
- Challenging teachers to think critically solving daily problems that arise with technology use
- Praising the efforts of teachers
- Communicating with teachers through e-mail, blogs and wiki's about projects and outcomes
- Communicating with outside stakeholders through email, flyers, and the ITV Studio

- Encouraging staff members to support each other
- Modeling the use of 21st century tools and resources

Assessment is another form and the last type of support we will discuss. Administrators that support the technology peer coaching program determine how the implementation is impacting teachers and students. Data must be used to make informed decisions. After review of the data on the effectiveness or outcomes of the program implementation, the team must be willing to make changes. If not, continuing to do the same thing will not produce a different result. However, without a leader that is willing to make the hard decisions, the team will not improve or move forward.

Development of assessment instruments can be achieved by the school leadership team or use of existing instruments may be available through the peer coaching program website.

Student achievement is another key for administrators to support technology peer coaching. Current research reveals technology integration does increase student achievement as many students are more engaged through the use of technology tools (Microsoft Peer Coaching Website, 2004).

In summary, administrators can empower teachers by supporting them with the resources needed to play TIG©. Teachers are players on this team just like athletic players. The TIG© and use of technology peer coaching strategies is a game that empowers teachers to engage students and enhance student achievement. Teachers, collaborating teachers, students, and administrators all play this game whether they know it or not. The question is: how well are you preparing your students for the 21st century? If you are not playing the TIG© with your students, we challenge you to do so! However, teachers need support to prepare students with 21st century skills. Our job as educational leaders is to continuously look for creative ways to provide support and implement a game plan for teachers and students where everyone wins! Stay tuned for our next book that will go in detail about the Technology Integration Game!

-Epilogue-

Supporting 21st Century Teaching and Learning…

We hope you quickly found that this is not another book promising that implementing peer coaching will increase student achievement dramatically and turn all schools into "A" schools. Peer coaching is however a model that can support educators as they embrace 21st century teaching and learning. The peer coaching strategies will enable educators to implement projects with students using technology tools to provide a real world education. Teachers who implement peer coaching will find that the support they need to engage in 21st century teaching and learning is a plus. Even if schools are earning "A's" or "B's" the question is: are you challenging students and preparing them for the 21st century? We can promise you that if you will take a long hard look at the ways you are engaging ALL students, you will realize that educators must work together just like athletic teams. We believe it is the only way we will win the learning game.

We have provided a glimpse of what it will take to help teachers embrace 21st century teaching and learning. The Partnership for 21st Century has provided the framework as a guide to assist schools. To help meet the standards the Partnership for 21st century has developed, we believe Peer Coaching is a powerful model that empowers teachers to communicate, collaborate, and build a community of teacher leaders who are ready to meet the challenge. If schools begin to envision themselves as athletic teams, we all can be on winning teams that are succeeding with students.

Most Americans understand sports and the desire to win the game. Schools that embrace the same desire can win at the game of learning. Technology Peer Coaching meets all of the 21st century professional development standards and the *Process* and *Context* National Staff Development Council Standards. Peer coaching empowers schools to develop teams of teachers who lead others transforming teaching and learning one classroom at a time.

If your school does not have a professional development model that provides ongoing, long term, sustained support for teachers, we have found that Technology Peer Coaching is a very effective model. Technology Peer Coaching meets the needs of all teachers regardless of what content area they teach. This is true as all content areas now receive online resources and materials to enhance learning in the classroom. Teachers should also be trained to integrate content across disciplines to provide a real world educational experience for our students. This is an exciting time in educational history and we challenge you to let us know how you are embracing 21st century teaching and learning. Stay tuned for our next book on the Technology Integration Game (TIG©), as it will provide details on ways schools can use peer coaching strategies to engage students in the game of learning. We will also discuss how administrators and teachers can hit home runs with students to win the learning game!

BIBLIOGRAPHY

Becker, Jean M. "Peer Coaching for Improvement of Teaching and Learning." http://www.teachersnetwork.org/tnpi/research/growth.becker.htm January 14, 2007.

Brainy Quotes Website. Tony Robbins Quote. Retrieved July 10, 2007, from http://www.brainyquote.com/quotes/authors/t/tony_robbins.html

Collins, D. (1997). Achieving Your Vision of Professional Development. Greensboro, NC: SouthEastern Regional Vision for Education.

Covey, Stephen R.. Seven Habits of Highly Effective People. New York: Fireside Books, 1989.

Darling-Hammond, L. (1999), "Teacher Learning that Supports Student Learning." Retrieved January 14, 2007 from http://www.edutopia.org/php/article.php?id=Art_478&key=238

Joyce, Bruce. "Staff Development Awareness Conference", Columbia, SC, January 1987.

National Staff Development Council Website. (2005). Retrieved January 14, 2007 from http://www.nsdc.org/standards/index.cfm

The Partnership for 21st Century Skills Website. (2004). Framework for 21st Century Learning. Retrieved September 1, 2007, from http://www.21stcenturyskills.org/index.php?option=com_content&task=view&id=254&Itemid=120

Peer Coaching Website. (2004). Coaching Cycle. Retrieved August 30, 2007, from http://pc.innovativeteachers.com/mpc_web/PeerCoaching/pc_programs.aspx

Peer Coaching Website. (2004). Coaching Models. Retrieved August 11, 2007, from http://pc.innovativeteachers.com/mpc_web/PeerCoaching/pc_coachingmodels.aspx

Rogers, E. M. (1995). *Diffusion of innovations (4th ed.)*. New York: Free Press.

Surpuriya, T. & Jordan, M. (1997). Teacher Burnout. Retrieved September 20, 2007 from http://weeklywire.com/ww/10-27-97/memphis_cvr.html

Appendix A

NSDC's Standards for Staff Development

(Revised, 2001)

Context Standards

Staff development that improves the learning of all students:

- Organizes adults into learning communities whose goals are aligned with those of the school and district. (Learning Communities)
- Requires skillful school and district leaders who guide continuous instructional improvement. (Leadership)
- Requires resources to support adult learning and collaboration. (Resources)

Process Standards

Staff development that improves the learning of all students:

- Uses disaggregated student data to determine adult learning priorities, monitor progress, and help sustain continuous improvement. (Data-Driven)
- Uses multiple sources of information to guide improvement and demonstrate its impact. (Evaluation)
- Prepares educators to apply research to decision making. (Research-Based)
- Uses learning strategies appropriate to the intended goal. (Design)
- Applies knowledge about human learning and change. (Learning)
- Provides educators with the knowledge and skills to collaborate. (Collaboration)

Content Standards

Staff development that improves the learning of all students:

- Prepares educators to understand and appreciate all students, create safe, orderly and supportive learning environments, and hold high expectations for their academic achievement. (Equity)
- Deepens educators' content knowledge, provides them with research-based instructional strategies to assist students in meeting rigorous academic standards, and prepares them to use various types of classroom assessments appropriately. (Quality Teaching)
- Provides educators with knowledge and skills to involve families and other stakeholders appropriately. (Family Involvement)

Appendix B

21ˢᵗ CENTURY STANDARDS & SKILLS

21ST CENTURY STUDENT OUTCOMES:

The elements described in this section as "21st century student outcomes" are the skills, knowledge and expertise students should master to succeed in work and life in the 21st century.

1. Core Subjects and 21st Century Themes

2. Learning and Innovation Skills

- Creativity and Innovation Skills
- Critical Thinking and Problem Solving Skills
- Communication and Collaboration Skills

3. Information, Media and Technology Skills

- Information Literacy
- Media Literacy
- ICT Literacy

4. Life and Career Skills

- Flexibility & Adaptability
- Initiative & Self-Direction
- Social & Cross-Cultural Skills
- Productivity & Accountability

- Leadership & Responsibility

21ST CENTURY SUPPORT SYSTEMS:

The elements described below are the critical systems necessary to ensure student mastery of 21st century skills. 21st century standards, assessments, curriculum, instruction, professional development and learning environments must be aligned to produce a support system that produces 21st century outcomes for today's students.

Reprinted with permission of The Partnership for 21st Century Skills
© 2004 PARTNERSHIP FOR 21ST CENTURY SKILLS

Appendix C

21st Century Professional Development

- Highlights ways teachers can seize opportunities for integrating 21st century skills, tools and teaching strategies into their classroom practice — and help them identify what activities they can replace/de-emphasize.
- Balances direct instruction with project-oriented teaching methods
- Illustrates how a deeper understanding of subject matter can actually enhance problem-solving, critical thinking, and other 21st century skills.
- Enables 21st century professional learning communities for teachers that models the kinds of classroom learning that best promotes 21st century skills for students
- Cultivates teachers' ability to identify students' particular learning styles, intelligences, strengths and weaknesses
- Helps teachers develop their abilities to use various strategies (such as formative assessments) to reach diverse students and to create environments that support differentiated teaching and learning

- Supports the continuous evaluation of students' 21st century skills development
- Encourages knowledge sharing among communities of practitioners, using face-to-face, virtual and blended communications
- Uses a scaleable and sustainable model of professional development

Appendix D

The Coaching Cycle

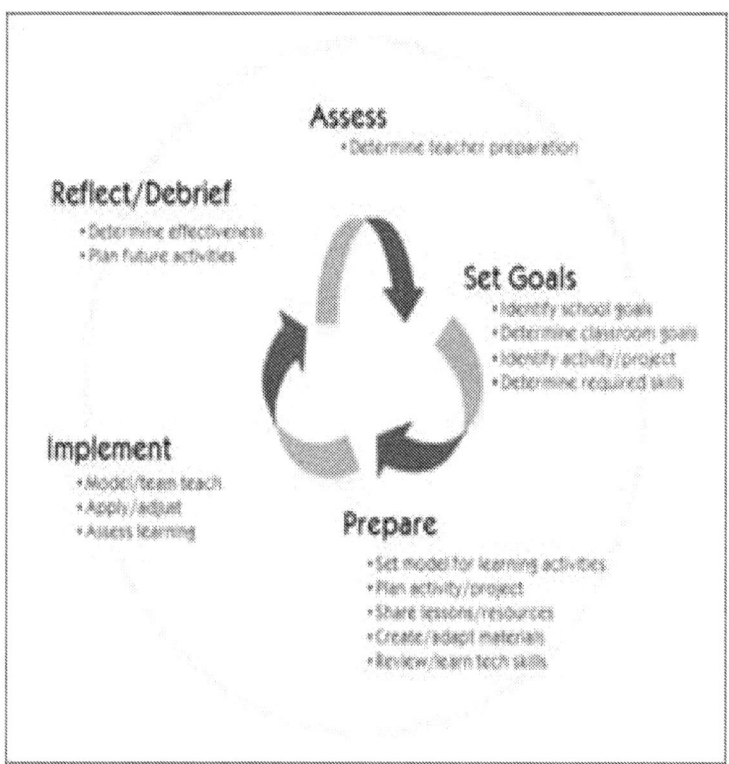

"Used with the permission of the Puget Sound Center for Teaching, Learning and Technology."

Peer Coaching Resources

http://techcoach.memphis.edu/ (Technology Coach handbook developed by University of Memphis)

http://cse.edc.org/products/teacherleadership/mentoring.asp (Education Development Center - Resources for Teacher Leadership)

http://www.madison.k12.wi.us/tnl/tech/teacherleaders.htm (Dane County Online Learning Consortium – Teacher Leaders)

http://www.nsdc.org/library/publications/jsd/feger252.cfm (How to develop a coaching eye. – Article – National Staff Development Council Website)

http://www.annenberginstitute.org/images/Coaching.pdf (Coaching - A Strategy For Developing Instructional Capacity, developed by the Annenberg Institute for School Reform)

http://www.my-ecoach.com/coaching/ (My e-Coach Website)

http://www.cognitivecoaching.com/whycc.htm (Center for Cognitive Coaching)

http://www.trngedu.com/peercoch.html (Training and Consulting Institute – 21st Century Leadership Skills for Peer Coaches)

http://www.teachermentors.com/RSOD%20Site/PeerCoach/CoachLinks.html

(Best Practices Resources for Peer Coaches)

http://pc.innovativeteachers.com/mpc_web/default.aspx (Peer Coaching Program Sponsored by Microsoft)

http://www.pugetsoundcenter.org/edLAB/peer_coaching_program.html (Puget Sound Center for Teaching, Learning, and Technology)

About the Authors

Virginia Richard works for Polk County Schools, School Technology Services, a department within the Information Systems and Technology Division, where she has been a Technology Specialist since 2003. She is also a Florida Master Digital Educator, a Technology Peer Coach Facilitator and manages a host of other district technology implementations for teachers and administrators. Virginia currently lives in Lakeland, Florida. Her hobbies are writing, reading, exploring and using cutting edge technology tools and when she has time, relaxing on the beach.

Kay Teehan is a Media Specialist at Bartow Middle School and adjunct instructor at Florida Southern College. She is a Florida Master Digital Educator, a Technology Peer Coach, and a National Board Certified Teacher. Kay lives in Lakeland, Florida with her husband, Larry. Her hobbies are writing, using and teaching others about technology applications, and reading. Her first book is titled: <u>Digital Storytelling: In and Out of the Classroom.</u>

www.ingramcontent.com/pod-product-compliance
Lightning Source LLC
Chambersburg PA
CBHW020807160426
43192CB00006B/471